ROMANIA

An Encyclopedic Survey

Second Edition

MERONIA

Editura Meronia

Bucharest, 1999

Editor: Horia C. Matei

Texts: Jana Balacciu-Matei, Caterina Radu

Translation into English:
Gabriela Dolgu, Ioana Ieronim
Supervision of the English version:
Christopher and Kathryn Frost

Text editing: Caterina Radú

Layout: Alexandru-Ion Radu
Cover: Corneliu Coterbic

Photos: Scarlat R. Arion, Alexandru Brumărescu, Constantin Dina, Mihai Oroveanu, Martin Rill, Georgeta Stoica, Emanuel Tânjală, Radu Vintilescu, Editura Enciclopedică, Editura Meronia, Filmex, Fundația Culturală Română, Muzeul Național de Artă al României, Oficiul Național pentru Documentare și Expoziții de Artă, Rompres, Teatrul German din Timișoara, Teatrul Maghiar din Cluj-Napoca, Teatrul Național din Craiova

Cartography: Cezar Melamedman

© **Meronia Publishers Ltd, Bucharest, Romania**

Printed by Edimpress Camro, Bucharest, Romania

ISBN 973–98844–5–8

CONTENTS

Cisnădie, a mediaeval town in Transylvania

Trying to describe Romania in one sentence is a hopeless exercise. Any statement about it has to be cushioned by a 'but'. In terms of area and population, Romania is a middle-sized country of the European continent. But it is the largest in the region of Southeastern Europe, a position which holds exciting promises for the future and awesome responsibilities right now. Geographically, it is located in the center of Europe, at the intersection of the continent's three great regions: Central Europe, Eastern Europe and the Balkan Peninsula. It actually belongs to none, but shares traditions, accomplishments and disappointments with each of them.

The Romanians are a Latin people speaking a Romance language like the French, the Italians, the Spanish, and the Portuguese. But, since it developed in the Eastern half of the Roman Empire, it remained a Latin island surrounded by peoples having other origins. Among the Latin nations, the Romanians are the only people who embraced the Eastern Christian faith, while proudly preserving their Roman heritage. When, in 1859, Romania became a nation-state, its emergence was shaped by the established patterns of Western Europe. At the conclusion of World War I, the ages-old Romanian dream came true: all Romanian territories were brought within the boundaries of one state. But in the aftermath of World War II, the Romanians, like other nations which fell under Soviet rule, had to live through the most disastrous utopian social experiment of the century. Then, in December 1989, the people of Romania rose against the communist regime and restored the blessings of democracy.

Romania is now facing a new historical challenge in a painful transition to functioning democracy and market economy. Despite enormous difficulties, the people of Romania are determined to write this new chapter in the country's history as a part of the European and Atlantic structures. Romania has undertaken to play a consistent role as a factor of stability and consensus building in a conflict-ridden region. It has engaged in a meaningful open dialogue with the world trying to communicate the values of its own cultural heritage. There are things to be seen in Romania. Visitors are welcomed with traditionally Romanian hospitality. This book aims to show that getting to know Romania better is an experience worth trying.

Romania and the new European geopolitical context

GENERAL INFORMATION

OFFICIAL NAME. ROMÂNIA (ROMANIA in English, ROUMANIE in French, RUMÄNIEN in German). This name was adopted in 1862, after the foundation of the nation-state through the union of the Romanian principalities of Wallachia and Moldavia in 1859. International abbreviation: RO.

GEOGRAPHICAL LOCATION. State situated in SE Central Europe, north of the Balkan Peninsula, on the Lower Danube, bordering on the Black Sea. Lying between 43°37'07" and 48°15'06" latitude north and 20°15'44" and 29°41'24" longitude east.

NEIGHBORS. Romania borders on five states: the Republic of Moldova (681.3 km.) in the northeast and east, Ukraine (649.4 km.) in the north and east, Bulgaria (631.3 km.) in the south, Yugoslavia (546.4 km.) in the southwest and Hungary (444.0 km.) in the west. The sixth neighbor is the Black Sea (193.5 km.).

AREA. 238,391 sq. km., comparable to Britain's area, which makes this country rank 13th in Europe and 80th in the world. Romania has an oval shape, the west-to-east straight line measuring 735 km. while the north-to-south one measures 530 km.

NATIONAL FLAG (proportion 3/2). Three equal vertical stripes of red, yellow and blue.

NATIONAL COAT OF ARMS (since 1992). An eagle holding a cross in its beak and a sword and a scepter in its talons, plus the symbols of the historical provinces of Wallachia, Moldavia, Transylvania, the Banat, Oltenia and Dobrudja.

Romania's national flag and coat of arms

STATE ANTHEM (since 1990). *Awake, Ye, Romanian*, with lyrics by Andrei Mureşanu (1816-1863) and music by Anton Pann (1796-1854).

NATIONAL DAY (since 1990). December 1, the anniversary of the Great Assembly held at Alba Iulia in 1918, which decided on Transylvania's union with Romania, a moment symbolizing the union of all Romanians in a single state.

LEGAL HOLIDAYS. January 1 and 2 (New Year), Easter Monday, May Day, December 1 (the national day), December 25 and 26 (Christmas).

STANDARD TIME. East European zone time (GMT+2 hours). Daylight saving time (GMT+3 hours) applies from March to October.

WEIGHTS AND MEASURES. Metric system in force since 1866.

CURRENCY (since 1867). The *Leu* (plural *lei*), with the *Ban* (plural *bani*) as subdivision (1 *leu*=100 *bani*). 1 US$=15,619 lei;

The Romanian Athenaeum, the emblem of Bucharest

1 DM=8,326 lei; 1 Ł=25,036 lei; 1 F.Fr.=2,482 lei; 1 Euro = 16,284 lei; 100 Yen=12,911 lei (June 1, 1999).

PHYSICAL FEATURES. The Carpathian Mountains occupy 31% of the country's area, the hills and plateaus hold 36%, while the plains account for 33% of Romania's total area. Maximum elevation: Moldoveanu Peak (2,544 m.) in the Făgăraş range of the Southern Carpathians.

CLIMATE. Temperate-continental with four seasons. In winter the average temperature is -3°C, while in summer the temperature averages 22-24°C. Average annual rainfall: ca. 640 mm.

AREA DISTRIBUTION. Arable area (39.2%), forests (28%), pastures and hayfields (20.3%), vineyards and vine nurseries (2.5%), waters and ponds (3.7%), buildings, roads and railways (6.1%).

Pope John Paul II in Bucharest together with Romania's President Emil Constantinescu and with the Patriarch of the Romanian Orthodox Church Teoctist (May 1999)

ENVIRONMENTAL PROTECTION. Romania has 810 protected areas, totaling 1,200,000 hectares; three of them are biosphere reserves (the Danube Delta, the Retezat Massif and Pietrosul Rodnei) and 14 are national parks.

POPULATION. 22,489,000 (ranked 10th in Europe and 43rd in the world). 55% of the population lives in the urban environment and 45% in the rural one. Population density: 94.3 inhabitants per sq.km. (ranked 26th in Europe and 74th in the world). Birth rate 10.5‰, death rate 13.2‰, natural growth -2.7‰. Life expectancy: 69.05 years for men and 73.09 for women. Population structure by age: 0-14 years (19.2%), 15-59 years

(62.3%), 60 years and over (18.5%). There are 6.5 marriages and 1.5 divorces per thousand population.

ETHNIC STRUCTURE. According to the 1992 census, 89.4% of the total population was Romanian and 10.6% was made up of ethnic minorities. There were 1,624,959 Hungarians (7.1%), 401,087 Gypsies (1.7%), 119,462 Germans (0.5%), 65,764 Ukrainians (0.3%), 8,955 Jews (0.04%), a.o.

RELIGION. The 1992 census indicated the following religious structure: 19,802,389 Eastern Orthodox (86.8%); 1,161,942 Roman-Catholic (5%); 802,454 Reformed (3.5%); 223,327 Greek-Catholic (1%); 220,824 Pentecostal (1%); 109,462 Baptist (0.5%); 77,546 Adventist (0.3%); 76,708 Unitarian (0.3%); 55,928 Muslim (0.2%); 49,963 Church of Christ (0.2%); 39,119 Augustan Evangelical (0.2%); 28,141 Old Rite Church (0.1%); 21,221 Presbyterian Evangelical (0.1%); 56,329 other denominations (0.2%); 34,645 without any religious affiliations (0.15%).

OFFICIAL LANGUAGE. Romanian. The easternmost representative of the Romance languages, Romanian is a continuation of the Latin spoken in ancient times in Dacia and Moesia, provinces of the Roman Empire. A 31-letter Latin

Arieșeni village in the Apuseni Mountains

alphabet is in use. Ethnic minorities can use their language in school, administration, the judiciary, and so on. Hungarian is spoken by the largest ethnic minority. English, French, and German are widely used.

LITERACY RATE. 98%.

ADMINISTRATIVE DIVISIONS. Communes, towns and cities, counties. Romania has 263 towns (80 of which are municipalities) and 2,686 communes (with 13,285 villages), comprised in 41 counties. The capital city, Bucharest, has the status of a county. A county has an average area of 5,800 sq.km. and an average population of 500,000.

CAPITAL CITY. Bucharest has a population of 2,021,000 and an area of 228 sq.km. In 1459 it became the princely seat of ruler Vlad Țepeș, in the 17th-19th centuries it was the capital of the principality of Wallachia, and since 1862 it has been the capital of Romania.

TOWNS AND CITIES. There are 263 towns, of which 25 have over 100,000 inhabitants, while eight have over 300,000. The latter group includes the capital and the following cities: Iași (350,000), Constanța (344,000), Cluj-Napoca (334,000), Galați

Sucevița Monastery in Northern Moldavia (16th c.)

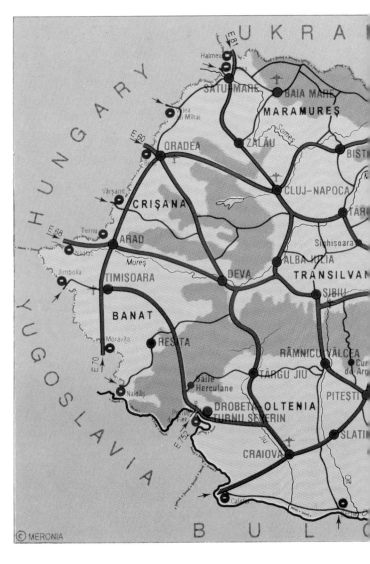

(331,000), Timişoara (327,000), Braşov (316,000) and Craiova (314,000).

AIRPORTS. The capital city has the airport of Bucharest-Otopeni for international traffic and Bucharest-Băneasa for domestic and international traffic. Another 15 cities have airports; Constanţa, Timişoara, Arad, Sibiu and Suceava also handle international traffic.

PORTS. Constanţa is the biggest port in the whole Black Sea area. Other seaports are Mangalia and Sulina. The main ports on the Danube are Orşova, Drobeta-Turnu Severin, Giurgiu, Călăraşi and Cernavodă. Three ports, Brăila, Galaţi and Tulcea, are both river and maritime ports.

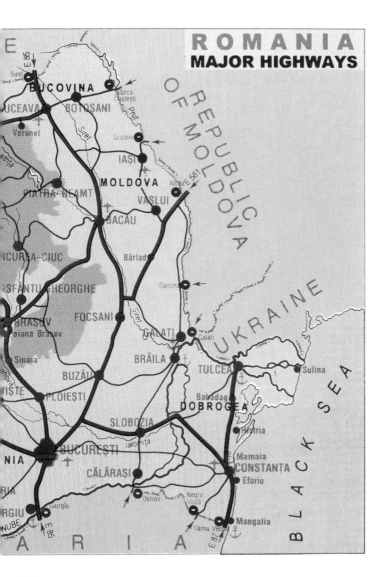

THE DANUBE-BLACK SEA CANAL. It was inaugurated in 1984. The canal is 64.2 km. long, 110-140 m. wide and 7-8.5 m. deep. Following the commissioning of the Main-Danube Canal in Germany, in 1992, the Danube-Black Sea Canal has been providing a direct connection between the Black Sea (Constanța) and the North Sea (Rotterdam).

GOVERNMENT. Under the 1991 Constitution, Romania is a parliamentary Republic. Legislative power is vested in the bicameral Parliament comprising the Chamber of Deputies (343 seats) and the Senate (143 seats). Parliament is elected by universal adult suffrage for a term of four years. Executive power is vested in the Government, headed by the Prime

Seagulls on the Black Sea coast

Minister appointed by the President. Members of the Government are appointed by the Prime Minister and approved by the Parliament. The Government is responsible to the Parliament. The President, who is also Commander-in-Chief of the Armed Forces, is elected by universal adult suffrage for at most two four-years terms. Head of the state: Emil Constantinescu (b. November 19, 1939), elected on November 17, 1996.

THE SHARE OF ECONOMIC SECTORS IN THE GDP. Industry (35%), agriculture and forestry (19%), services (34%), constructions (5%), other sectors (7%). Private business: 58% of the GDP.

GROSS DOMESTIC PRODUCT (1998). 338,670 billion lei. Per capita GDP: 15.05 million lei.

FOREIGN TRADE (1998). FOB export worth $ 8,299 million, CIF import worth $ 11,821 million. Main partners: Italy, Germany, France, and USA.

INTERNATIONAL RELATIONS. Romania has diplomatic relations with 176 states and is a member of the UN and all its bodies and specialized agencies. In 1993 this country became a member of the Council of Europe, in 1994 it was the first state in Eastern Europe to sign the Partnership for Peace with NATO and in 1995 it became an associate to the European Union.

THE LAND

Romania is a middle-sized country in Europe; by area it ranks 13th, and in terms of population it is the 10th in the continent. Actually, it lies in the center of Europe, as parallel of 45° latitude North, halfway between the Equator and the North Pole, intersects this country's territory close to Bucharest, the capital city. Passing near Bucharest is also the meridian of 25° longitude East, which marks the middle of distance between the Atlantic and the Ural Mountains, Europe's western and eastern limits.

Three geographical factors have decisively influenced the destiny of Romania's territory: the Carpathian Mountains, the Lower Danube and the Black Sea coast. The arch-shaped

"The Sphinx" in the Bucegi Massif, the Southern Carpathians

Winter and spring at the foot of the Carpathian Mountains

Carpathians delimited the three large historical regions in which the Romanians developed: the region lying inside the Carpathian arch and opening onto Central Europe, the region located east of the mountains and opening onto the North Black Sea, and the region south of the Carpathians which opens onto the Balkan Peninsula. The Danube, the second largest European river, and the only major river flowing from west to east, which separates the Carpathian space from the Balkan area, connects Central Europe to the Black Sea basin. The Romanian coast of the Black Sea has been a gate towards the Oriental world as well as towards the Mediterranean. Dobrudja, located between the Danube and the Black Sea, served in antiquity and in the Middle Ages as a corridor for the populations from the steppes of Eastern Europe and from north of the Black Sea who were advancing towards the Balkan Peninsula and further towards the Middle East. All these factors have turned Romania throughout history into a bridge between Central and Eastern Europe and the Balkan Peninsula and further towards the Middle East.

Were a person to render the nature of Romania in one word, this word would surely be harmony. Few countries of this size are blessed with such a diverse, yet complementary, terrain. Viewed from an airplane, the Romanian territory looks like a great amphitheater, with mountains, hills and plains, each taking up about one third of the surface, concentrically disposed.

Out of a total length of 1,500 km, 910 km of the Carpathian Mountains are in Romania. Teeming with a variety of landscapes, the arch-shaped range towers over the whole land. Although not extremely high on the whole, the Southern Carpathians are the highest. Four peaks rise over 2,500 m, the highest one being Moldoveanu in the Făgăraş Massif

(2,544 m). They offer an alpine landscape with jagged crests, needle ridges and many glacier lakes. That is why they were called "the Transylvanian Alps." However, most of their peaks are flattened or slightly undulated plateaus, with alpine pastures and meadows, extensively used for grazing sheep or cattle in summertime. In the Western and Eastern Carpathians, which are lower and have gentler slopes, many passes provide convenient inland corridors. The valleys and depressions of 200-400 m altitude form genuine interior plains. One of them, Țara Hațegului, in the Western Carpathians, harbored the nucleus of the old Dacian State. On the high, but large and flat plateaus, permanent human settlements developed as high as 1,400-1,600 m. In such isolated places traditional customs and culture have been preserved almost

Sunset on the Danube, at Sulina

Landscape in the Southern Carpathians

unaltered. The Eastern Carpathians feature a combination of structures that is indeed rare in the world. Here there are three parallel ranges of different structures: in the west, a volcanic one, the longest volcanic chain in Europe; in center, one of hard rock; and in the east, one of sedimentary, less resistant, rock. Huge gold, silver, salt and marble deposits were known and much coveted by many in ancient times. The Romans, who eventually conquered the territory, started the intensive mining of these resources. Subsequently, centuries of large-scale exploitation sensibly reduced the deposits.

Later, oil and methane were discovered and started being exploited. Beginning in 1857, Romania was for 120 years Europe's second biggest producer of crude oil and one of the world's major producers of methane gas.

The Carpathians encircle the Transylvanian Tableland (400-600 m) like a crown, being in their turn surrounded by hills,

Sunflower field in the Moldavian Tableland

which rise up to 1,000 m. To the east and south-east there are the Moldavian and the Dobrudja Tablelands (400-600 m), to the east and south the Sub-Carpathians (500-1000 m.), and to the west the Western Hills, which do not rise above 300-400 m. The Sub-Carpathians are very rich in salt deposits, which make the country one of the first European producers.

In the south and west of the country, the low and extremely flat plains make available ample opportunity for agriculture especially for cultivation of wheat and maize. The Romanian Plain, along the Danube, in the south, is the most fertile region of the country, formerly known as its major breadbasket. In the west, the large Western Plain also provides best opportunities for farming and vine growing.

Peasant from Sibiu area

The Danube enters this country through a spectacular gorge (Baziaş–Drobeta-Turnu Severin Pass), the longest (144 km.) in Europe and the most powerful source of energy on the continent. Over 1964-1971, Romania and Yugoslavia jointly built here the hydropower and navigation system Iron Gates I, with a big hydropower station supplying 2,100 MW (of which 1,050 to Romania). In 1985, the second hydropower station, Iron Gates II, of 216 MW, also built jointly by Romania and Yugoslavia, was commissioned.

More than one third of the Danube (1,075 km.) slithers through the country from west to east. On a distance of 750 km. it forms Romania's southern border, first with Yugoslavia, and then with Bulgaria. The river empties into the Black Sea

Pasture at the foot of the Făgăraș Mountains

through three arms (Chilia, Sulina and Sfântu Gheorghe) which enclose a delta of 5,050 sq. km. of which 4,340 sq.km. on Romanian territory, the rest belonging to neighboring Ukraine.

The Danube Delta, the largest delta in Europe, is mostly made of submersed terrain, channels, and islets that combine into a unique landscape.

Romania is a well-watered country. The nature of the Romanian relief resulted in a radial pattern of drainage, with most rivers flowing from the Carpathians and pouring their waters, directly or through tributaries, into the Danube. The greatest are: the Mureș (768 km. in Romania out of its total length) and the Someș (386 km. on Romania's territory), in the west, the Prut (716 km in Romania) and the Siret (596 km. on this country's territory) in the east, the Olt (737 km.) and the Ialomița (410 km.) in the south. Concentrated in the volcanic chain of the Eastern Carpathians, there are a great number of mineral and thermal springs, with curative properties, around which many all-season spas have developed. Natural sparkling mineral water is a great resource that still awaits efficient economic exploitation. Moreover, salty lakes, also to be found in the hills, as well as in the plains, are largely used as spas.

The 3,500 lakes, of which over 2,000 are natural, cover only one per cent of the country's surface; generally they are small and different in nature. The saline lagoons on the coast of the Black Sea are in fact the largest lakes (the biggest one is Razelm, 415 sq. km.) in Romania. Also, there are over 200 wonderful glacial lakes on the high plateaus of the Retezat and Făgăraş Mountains in the Southern Carpathians.

Romania has a temperate-continental climate, with four clearly defined seasons. Temperatures average –3°C in winter and 22-24°C in summer, but the highest temperature ever recorded reached 44.4°C in the southern Bărăgan Plain in 1951, while the lowest -38.5°C near Braşov, in 1942. Weather slightly varies in different parts of the country because of both relief and external atmospheric influences. Thus, in the west, where a slight oceanic (Atlantic) influence is felt, and in the southwest, where there is a Mediterranean influence, winters are usually mild and the precipitation is abundant. In the east, where the excessive East-European climate is strongly felt, winters are cooler and summers are hotter. The average precipitation is 640 mm annually, with larger amounts in the mountains (over 1,000 mm) and smaller amounts in the plains (500 mm) and the Danube Delta (400 mm).

In the past, forests covered much of the country's area, but now only little over a quarter of the surface is forested. On the plains, oak forests and steppe vegetation were depleted, as space was cleared for farming. In the hills, where beech and oak forests are common, there are many vineyards and orchards. Evergreen coniferous forests prevail at altitudes over 1,200 m.

Wildlife is still one of the richest and most varied in Europe, boasting some rare and even unique species on the continent. The Carpathian deers, brown bears, lynx, wolves and wild boars populate the mountains, while chamois and mountain eagles can be found in the alpine

Jupiter resort on the Black Sea coast

"Babele" rocks in the Bucegi Mountains

zones. In the hills and plains live hares, foxes, wild boars, roes, then woodpeckers, partridge, quail and many other species of birds. Romania is one of the few countries in the world where the number of wolves is big enough to permit hunting. The Danube Delta remains one of most spectacular bird sanctuaries, with more than 300 native species and migrating waterfowl. The greatest colonies of pelicans in Europe, white and black swans and egrets, wild ducks and geese are to be found here. Rivers and lakes teem with fish (carp, sheatfish, pike, zander, etc.), and the lower Danube and the Black Sea are replete with sturgeon, providing precious caviar.

In order to preserve this harmony of the Romanian landscape, environmental protection began early in the 20th century. The first law was passed in 1930 and, one year later, a Commission for the Protection of Nature Monuments was established and still functions under the Romanian Academy. There is also a government department that works out programs to prevent excessive exploitation of the country's natural resources. Nevertheless, industrialization and large-scale agriculture, mainly in recent decades, have impacted the harmonious biological diversity. Today there are 810 protected areas across the country, covering 5.3% of its surface (1,200,000 ha). Three of them, the Retezat National Park in the Southern Carpathians (created in 1935), the Danube Delta (1930) and the Rodna reservation in the Southern Carpathians (1932) were, as of 1990, included as biosphere reserves on the UNESCO World Heritage list.

Wooden church in Șurdești village (18th c.)

COUNTY	AREA (sq km)	POPULATION (1.1.1998)	COUNTY SEAT	POPULATION (1.1.1998)
Alba	6,242	401,687	Alba Iulia	72,405
Arad	7,754	478,108	Arad	185,272
Argeș	6,862	675,727	Pitești	187,558
Bacău	6,621	747,645	Bacău	210,042
Bihor	7,544	625,429	Oradea	223,190
Bistrița-Năsăud	5,355	326,383	Bistrița	87,169
Botoșani	4,986	460,973	Botoșani	128,888
Brașov	5,363	634,881	Brașov	315,843
Brăila	4,766	388,816	Brăila	234,201
Buzău	6,103	508,459	Buzău	149,025
Caraș-Severin	8,520	360,627	Reșița	94,320
Călărași	5,088	332,494	Călărași	77,819
Cluj	6,674	724,605	Cluj-Napoca	333,607
Constanța	7,071	746,988	Constanța	343,986
Covasna	3,710	231,172	Sfântu Gheorghe	67,108
Dâmbovița	4,054	554,161	Târgoviște	99,137
Dolj	7,414	749,019	Craiova	314,437
Galați	4,466	642,337	Galați	332,154
Giurgiu	3,526	298,242	Giurgiu	73,260
Gorj	5,602	397,668	Târgu Jiu	98,897
Harghita	6,639	343,467	Miercurea-Ciuc	47,073
Hunedoara	7,063	536,165	Deva	77,259
Ialomița	4,453	304,803	Slobozia	56,913
Iași	5,476	826,307	Iași	349,544
Ilfov	1,593	277,357	Buftea	19,807
Maramureș	6,304	533,162	Baia Mare	149,735
Mehedinți	4,933	325,857	Turnu Severin	118,734
Mureș	6,714	602,426	Târgu Mureș	165,835
Neamț	5,896	583,687	Piatra-Neamț	125,050
Olt	5,498	513,266	Slatina	87,608
Prahova	4,716	862,457	Ploiești	253,068
Satu Mare	4,418	392,265	Satu Mare	130,573
Sălaj	3,864	258,717	Zalău	71,580
Sibiu	5,432	445,281	Sibiu	170,038
Suceava	8,553	712,854	Suceava	118,670
Teleorman	5,790	465,053	Alexandria	59,308
Timiș	8,697	684,506	Timișoara	326,958
Tulcea	8,499	265,349	Tulcea	96,813
Vaslui	5,318	462,385	Vaslui	79,658
Vâlcea	5,765	432,980	Râmnicu Vâlcea	119,581
Vrancea	4,857	391,263	Focșani	99,527
Bucharest	228	2,021,065	Bucharest	2,021,065

THE PEOPLE

The Romanians have continuously inhabited the selfsame geographical space to this day. This is the space that their forefathers, the Dacians, populated as early as the second millennium BC. Romanians were always the main population in the territories of today's Romania. Before the 1859 Union, in Wallachia and Moldavia they represented nine-tenths of the total population. In Transylvania, during its inclusion in other states, they were the largest ethnic group, some two-thirds of the total population.

Romanians are the only Latin people of Orthodox faith. Christianity spread here during the Roman rule in Dacia. Various sources agree that Apostle Andrew came and preached here, fathering Christianization. As faith was essential in the life of the medieval man, the Christian local people had very few contacts with the migratory, pagan populations that crossed their territory. Thus, Christianity helped preserve the Latin character of the local people. A great Romanian archaeologist, Vasile Pârvan, expressed this historical fact in a memorable way, saying that "the Romanian people was born Christian." The metropolitanates of Wallachia (set up in 1359) and of Moldavia (1401) were subordinated to the patriarch in Constantinople. The Romanian Orthodox Church became autocephalous, i.e. governed by its own metropolitan, in 1885, and was raised to the rank of patriarchate in 1925.

In Transylvania, after its conquest by the Hungarians and its incorporation, as a *voievodat*, in the Hungarian Kingdom, the official religion was Catholicism. However, the Romanians

Fortune with Pontos (AD 2nd-3rd c.)

Roadside cross in Maramureș

Gârbova village in Alba county

preserved their Orthodox faith. This loyalty cost them their public rights and relegated them to a lower social status. Only in 1697-1701, after Transylvania's inclusion in the Hapsburg (later Austro-Hungarian) Empire, did part of the Orthodox clergy join the Catholic Church. They accepted the Papal primacy, while retaining the Orthodox rite. That is how the Greek-Catholic Church came into being. The main benefit was recognition of its rights on equal terms with those of the other denominations. The Greek-Catholic clergy used this gain in the struggle for the Romanians' emancipation. In 1948, the communist authorities banned the Greek-Catholic Church and forced it to merge with the Romanian Orthodox Church. In 1990, in the wake of the communist dictatorship collapse, the Greek-Orthodox Church regained its right to existence.

The Romanians Abroad

Estimates put the number of the Romanians abroad somewhere between eight and ten million. There are about four million Romanians who remained within the borders of other states, following territorial amputations suffered by Romania. They live east and north of the Prut river, in Ukraine and in the Republic of Moldova. The latter is practically another Romanian State, which won independence in 1991, after the dissolution of the USSR. In the Republic of Moldova the official language is Romanian, although it is called "Moldovan". Communities of Romanians are also present in Hungary, Yugoslavia and other neighboring countries. In different Balkan states there exist communities of Aromanians (or Macedo-Romanians), Megleno-Romanians and Istro-Romanians. They are descendants of the Romanians who lived south of the Danube and were dislodged by the massive Slavic wave in the 7th-8th centuries. Their number shrinks as they gradually lose their native tongue.

Emigration was not a large-scale phenomenon with the Romanians. In the inter-war years few people left or came here, the annual average standing at 2,000. The communist

Voronet Monastery in Northern Moldavia (15th-16th c.)

Little peasant girl from Bukovina

regime caused the biggest wave of emigration ever, nearly two million persons. The largest Romanian communities are to be found in Western Europe (Germany, France, Italy, Austria, Sweden and Spain) and in the United States and Canada. There are Romanians also in South America, Australia and New Zealand. In Asia, Romanians who lived in the former Soviet Union and were deported or forced to take jobs in Siberia, live now in Kazakhstan, Uzbekistan, Turkmenistan and Kyrgyzstan. Communism strictly forbade communication and free dialogue with the émigrés. After December 1989, the ties between the country and the Diaspora were at last resumed.

Ethnic Minorities

According to the latest census (1992), ethnic minorities stand for 10.6% of the total population. There are Hungarians (7.1%), Gypsies (1.7%), Germans (0.5%), Ukrainians (0.3%), Jews (0.04%) and others. The Constitution stipulates that "Romania is the common and indivisible homeland of its citizens, irrespective of race, nationality, ethnic origin, language, religion". The minorities may freely use their mother tongue in schools, administration, justice, media and culture. There are kindergartens, primary schools and secondary schools for Hungarians, Germans, Serbs, Ukrainians, Czechs,

Bulgarians, Turks a.o. There are 180 newspapers and magazines published in the languages of ethnic minorities, particularly in Hungarian and German. There are Hungarian theaters in Timişoara, Cluj-Napoca and Târgu-Mureş; there is a German one in Timişoara, and a Jewish theater in Bucharest. The national radio stations and television broadcast programs in the languages of ethnic minorities. UDMR, the ethnic party of the Hungarians, now takes part in the coalition government, and all the other minorities are represented in the Parliament.

The Hungarians settled down in Transylvania in the 11th-13th centuries; because their numbers were small, they brought here other ethnic groups and granted them privileges to make

Little peasant boy from Southern Transylvania

The St. Michael Cathedral in Cluj-Napoca (14th-15th c.)

them loyal to the Hungarian Crown. The first to come here were the Szecklers, an ethnically heterogeneous population, allied with the Hungarians and gradually assimilated by them. Ethnic Germans, later to be called Saxons, were brought to southern and eastern Transylvania. All the Hungarians and Saxons were Catholics. As the Reform gained ground in the 16th century, the Saxons embraced Lutheranism, while part of the Hungarians adhered to Calvinism and a small number became Unitarians. The Banat – a region in southwestern Romania, incorporated in the Hapsburg Empire in 1718 – was colonized in the 18th century by the House of Austria with Catholic Swabians, of German origin. German colonists settled also in Bukovina in the late 18th century. In Dobrudja, a region between the Danube and the Black Sea, communities of Turks and Tartars emerged during the Ottoman domination.

Other ethnic minorities were originally immigrants. In the Middle Ages, isolated groups of Gypsies, Armenians and Jews

Village in the Danube Delta

Woman peasant from Sibiel village, Sibiu county

Street in Braşov

Băile Herculane

Downtown Oradea

The St. Joseph Catholic Cathedral in Bucharest

The Mosque in Constanţa

settled down here. The Jewish communities grew rapidly at the end of the 19th century, through substantial immigration from the Tsarist and Hapsburg Empires, so that the Jews became the largest ethnic minority in Romania before the 1918 Union. The first census conducted in Romania after the Great Union, in 1930, recorded 722,000 Jews, a number almost equal with that of the Germans (Saxons and Swabians). A significant percentage of the nearly two million persons who left the country during the communist years were Germans, Jews and Armenians; these communities virtually disappeared after having existed in Romania for centuries. Two countries in particular have become new homelands for the minority groups that left Romania: Germany, for about 600,000 Saxons and Swabians, and Israel for 450,000 Jews. The communities of Jews, Saxons, Swabians, Armenians, Greeks, who were born and spiritually grew in the Romanian environment, have

The Armenian Church in Bucharest

The Jewish Temple in Bucharest

remained close to the language and culture of their country of origin, no matter where they went to live.

The City and the Village

In Romania the village was for a long time the main form of human community. Today 45% of the Romanians still live in the rural area, which is much more than the European average and double the American percentage. At present, there are 13,000 villages, each with a population ranging from a few hundred to a few thousand. Nevertheless, urban civilization has a long history in Romania. The first towns appeared more than 2500 years ago; they were colonies founded by the Greeks on the Black Sea coast: Histria, Callatis (today Mangalia) and Tomis

Easter eve at the Patriarchal Church in Bucharest

(the port-city of Constanța, the biggest in the Black Sea area). Tomis was the place were the great Roman poet, Ovid, was banished in AD 8 and spent his last nine years. For over one thousand years those colonies had a notable role in the commercial and cultural life in this part of the world. Then, under the Roman rule, urbanization was fast. Big cities developed on the place of ancient Dacian settlements, such as Apulum (today Alba Iulia), Napoca (today Cluj-Napoca), Drobeta (Drobeta-Turnu Severin) and others. Geographer Ptolemy's map shows 44 towns in Dacia in the second century AD. The waves of migration, which lasted almost one millennium, destroyed the cities and the urban life. The first medieval towns emerged as late as the 10th-12th centuries, at the crossroads of major trade routes, first in Transylvania and Dobrudja and then in Moldavia and Wallachia.

In Romania today there are 263 towns and cities. Bucharest, the former capital of Wallachia and then of the Romanian nation-state, with its two million inhabitants, is today the biggest city in the country and the second biggest in the region after Athens. Other important Romanian cities are: Iaşi, Cluj-Napoca, Constanţa, Craiova, Timişoara, Braşov and Galaţi.

The Romanian Family

In Romania the family continues to be a very important institution. Moreover, it has preserved its traditional structure. Cohabitation, a feature common to many Western European countries, is not frequent, and children are rarely born outside marriages. Though people start families at a relatively young age, divorces are fewer than the European or American average. Traditional family does not mean that the father works and the mother is a housewife. After the Second World War, that type of family practically disappeared. Men and women have equal employment opportunities and no discrimination is made in payment. Many women have achieved distinction in their careers in medicine, education, sciences or other fields. However, in the last few years, when the Romanians were confronted with unemployment, women have been more affected.

From the "Immortal" Dacians to Dacia Felix

The territory of present-day Romania was inhabited by Dacians, who were of Thracian origin. Greek historian Herodotus (fifth century BC) provides the first written account of their existence in this area when narrating the campaigns of Darius I against the Scythians of the north-Pontic steppes (513 BC). He says that the Dacians were the only ones who opposed Darius, as they were the bravest and the most righteous among the Thracians, and they believed they were immortals.

Dacia was rich and densely populated. In the seventh and sixth centuries BC Greeks had founded, on the Black Sea coast, the colonies of Histria, Tomis and Callatis. In the first century BC, King Burebista (ca 70 - ca 44 BC) united the Dacians in a state much larger than today's Romania and powerful enough to be a threat even to the Romans. Burebista, described as "the most powerful among all the kings that ever reigned in Thracia", imposed his rule over the Celts and controlled the Greek cities along the Black Sea coast. He intended to interfere in the Roman civil wars supporting Pompey against Julius Caesar. The latter was planning an expedition against the Dacians, but both rulers fell victim to conspiracies in the same year. After Burebista's death, the Dacian State lost much of its previous power and gradually fell under the influence of Rome. The impact of Roman civilization was felt throughout Dacian society, in its way of

The Hamangia Thinker and His Wife (5th millennium BC)

life and its customs. In the first century AD, King Decebal (AD 87–106) rebuilt a powerful Dacian State, which posed a threat to Rome. Frequent Dacian raids south of the Danube, and a war waged during Emperor Domitian's reign, only increased Decebal's power. The situation changed when Emperor Trajan (AD 98–117) came to the throne. He had strong motives to fight the Dacians: to avenge the defeats suffered by the Romans during Domitian's time, to eliminate the threat at the Danubian borders of the empire and to get hold of the vast gold and silver resources of the Dacians. The two wars (AD 101–102 and 105–106) ended with the defeat of the Dacians. Their capital, Sarmizegetusa, was captured and destroyed, while Decebal and other Dacian chieftains killed themselves to escape being paraded as captives in Rome. The Daco-Roman wars were depicted on Trajan's Column in Rome.

After AD 106 Dacia became a flourishing province of the Roman Empire, also called *Dacia felix.* There was a great

The Greek colony of Histria (7th c. BC)

influx of people from all over the Roman Empire into Dacia. The Dacians, who had remained in the province to live side by side with the colonists, soon began speaking Latin and adopting the Roman customs. The process of Romanization was advancing gradually but steadily. Under the pressure of the barbarian invasions, the Roman Empire withdrew its army and administration south of the Danube in AD 271-274.

After AD 300, for several centuries, successive migratory waves of Germanic, Turkic, Slavic or Mongolian origin crossed and plundered Romania's territory on their way to Byzantium or to the West. However, the Romanized local population preserved its Latin language and identity. Having penetrated in Dacia during the Roman administration, and having been strengthened by Latin-speaking missionaries coming from the Empire, Christianity had a major role in consolidating the Latin

The Dacian Rhyton at Poroina (3rd c. BC)   *Dacian nobleman (Roman sculpture)*

language and identity of the people. Gradually this population that assimilated small groups of barbarians, especially Slavs (who came here in the sixth-seventh centuries), evolved into a new distinct people – the Romanian one. The Romanians were more and more often mentioned in historical sources after AD 900 as *Vlachs*, which meant "Roman-related", but they called themselves *Romanian,* from the Latin *romanus.* The largest part of the Romanians came into being and continued living north of the Danube, in today's territory of Romania and the Republic of Moldova. Meanwhile, some small groups (Aromanians, Megleno-Romanians and Istro-Romanians) remained south of the Danube and still live in several Balkan states. The Romanian people developed within

*The Roman Triumphal Monument
of Adamclisi (AD 109)*

*Dacian golden helmet from Poiana
Cotofenești (4th c. BC)*

the Roman world. The ties with Constantinople, the capital of the Eastern Roman Empire, which soon surpassed Rome in importance, were never severed. When the Christian world split, the Romanians followed Constantinople and joined the Orthodox Church. Consequently, they emerged as the only Latin people in this area, isolated from all the other Latin ones, and became the only Latin people that belong to the Orthodox Church.

One People and Three States

The first state formations of the Romanians were recorded in the territory of present-day Romania in the 9th–10th centuries. Some of them, located in Transylvania, were conquered by the Hungarians in the 11th–13th centuries, and integrated into a *voievodat* of that kingdom. Then, following

Roman funeral stele at Alba Iulia (2nd-3rd c.)

The golden hoard of Pietroasa (4th c.)

the victory scored by the Turkish army at Mohács, in 1526, Hungary disintegrated, and in 1541 Transylvania became an autonomous principality under the suzerainty of the Ottoman Empire. Between 1688 and 1918 it was part of the Hapsburg Empire. South and east of the Carpathians, the Romanian states of Wallachia and, respectively, Moldavia emerged in the 14th century. They survived in spite of the expansionist tendencies of powerful neighbors. In the 15th century, Wallachia and Moldavia came under Ottoman rule, which lasted more than three centuries. However, unlike most Balkan countries, which were turned into provinces of the Ottoman Empire, the Romanian states managed to remain distinct Christian states and keep their own institutions.

During the Middle Ages, through the fight waged against the Ottoman Porte, the Romanians and their neighbors were real defenders of the European civilization. Princes Mircea

The princely belt clasp found at the princely church at "Curtea de Argeş" (14th c.)

the Old (1386-1418), Stephen the Great (1457-1504), Iancu of Hunedoara (1441-1456) and Michael the Brave (1593-1601) were heroes of that resistance throughout centuries. In 1599-1600, Michael the Brave briefly united the three Romanian countries, Wallachia, Moldavia and Transylvania, under his rule. Later generations honored him as a symbol of the Romanians' union. Vlad Dracula, nicknamed Țepeș (the Impaler), who ruled Wallachia between 1456 and 1462, became a controversial figure. Prince Vlad treated his enemies cruelly, so that his name, Dracula, was put in relation with

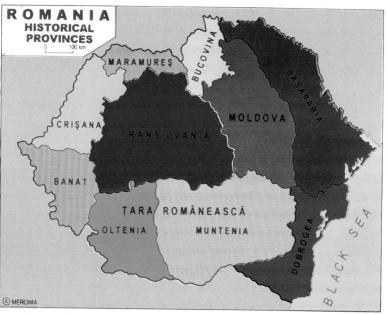

drac, which means devil. At the end of the 19th century, the Irish writer Bram Stoker wrote a novel vaguely inspired by the Romanian prince, and then fiction came to prevail over reality and the brave Wallachian prince became the notorious vampire!

The Modern Romanian Nation-State

In the Romanian countries, the 18th and 19th centuries were times of fast modernization and the beginning of the rise of national consciousness. The Romanians combined battle with clever diplomacy to gain recognition of their political and national rights. In Transylvania a revolt broke out in 1784; in Wallachia a revolution took place in 1821; and in 1848–1849 the European revolution erupted in all three Romanian countries. The ultimate goal pursued by the political forces was to found Romania, a state for all Romanians. The achievement of this objective often met with the opposition of the neighboring multinational empires that had annexed Romanian territories: the Hapsburg Empire (called Austria-Hungary as of 1867), the Ottoman Empire and the Tsarist Empire. However, the European context became more favorable in the latter half of the 19th century. In 1859 a major step toward the union was made through the double election of Alexandru Ioan Cuza as ruling prince of both Moldavia and Wallachia. The great powers soon recognized the new nation-state called Romania, with Bucharest as its capital city. The modernization policy of Alexandru Ioan Cuza (1859-1866) would then be furthered by Carol I of Hohenzollern-Sigmaringen (1866-1914). Under the latter's reign, Romania adopted an advanced Constitution (1866), the country's full independence was recognized following the Russian-Romanian-Turkish war of 1877–1878, and the country became a kingdom in 1881. It was a time of development and consolidation. Romania's progress was visible in every field, and its prestige continued to grow. At the beginning of the 19th century, the country was often referred to as "Belgium of the (European) East".

Soroca Fortress on the Dniester, built by Moldavian prince Petru Rareș (16th c.)

In the early 20th century, more than half of the Romanians lived under foreign rule - in the Austro-Hungarian Empire (Bukovina and Transylvania) and in Russia (Bessarabia). In World War I, with a view to fulfilling the national ideal of unity, Romania joined the Entente (1916), during the reign of King Ferdinand I (1914–1927). At the end of the war the big empires collapsed. In 1918, parliamentary bodies were democratically elected in the Romanian provinces that were part of the former

Cozia Monastery in the Olt Valley (14th c.)

empires. They decided on the union of those provinces with the Kingdom of Romania. In Chişinău on April 9, in Cernăuți on November 28, and at Alba Iulia on December 1, the Romanians of Bessarabia, Bukovina and Transylvania declared for the union of those provinces with the "motherland." The long-cherished national aspirations for unity were at last fulfilled due to the struggle fought by generations, and at the cost of 800,000 casualties of war. In 1919-1920, the peace treaties signed in France recognized the new Romania, one that contained all the Romanian territories within its borders. The country doubled in size and in population.

Romania Between the Two Wars

The decades between the world wars (1918–1939) saw great achievements that led to Romania's development into a

Hunedoara Castle (15th c.)

Romanian troops during the Pleven Siège (1877)

modern nation: universal suffrage, a radical agrarian reform, a new democratic Constitution. Economic upsurge resulted in a per capita GDP bigger than that of Greece or Portugal. Unfortunately, these achievements were cut short when the revisionist trends and the war preparations gained ground in Europe. After the outbreak of World War II, Romania, in 1940, lost a third of its territory. Through arbitrary acts dictated by the Soviet Union, Germany and Italy, Bessarabia and Northern Bukovina were annexed by the USSR, and a large part of Transylvania went to Hungary. In the wake of the political crisis that followed, King Carol II (1930-1940) abdicated in favor of his son Mihai I, but the power was actually taken over by General, then Marshal, Ion Antonescu (1940-1944). Romania's situation was now at its worst. Isolated from its traditional allies, France and Britain, and fearing the communist peril, the country had to accept an alliance with Germany. Romania

The coat of arms of the
Romanian Kingdom (1921)

The kings of Romania: Carol I,
Ferdinand I, Carol II and Mihai I

Bucharest. Calea Victoriei in 1930

entered World War II in 1941 on Germany's side, hoping to retrieve its Russian-occupied territories. The subsequent course of events led to the downfall of Antonescu's dictatorship on August 23, 1944. Romania declared war on Germany and joined the allied forces. Until the end of the war (May 9, 1945), Romania fought against Germany and its allies. Nevertheless, the Paris Peace Conference (1946-1947) did not recognize Romania's co-belligerent status, nor did it return Bessarabia and Northern Bukovina to the country. However, Romania's right over northern Transylvania was recognized.

Behind the Iron Curtain

With Soviet troops stationed in its territory, Romania's course of development was abruptly changed. With the rapid rise to power of the Communist Party, backed by Soviet

December 1989

authorities, the country turned away from Europe and toward Moscow. The dismantling of the existing structures came in rapid sequence. Parliamentary elections were rigged (1946), King Mihai I was forced to abdicate (1947), political parties were banned, the economy was nationalized (1948), and agriculture was collectivized (1949-1962). A ruthless, Soviet-type repression machinery (prisons, the labor camp at the Danube-Black Sea Canal) was used to eradicate the political and cultural elite of Romania. Slogans and the promise of a better life were used to attract the grass roots. The '60s seemed to bring a slight "thaw" and especially some departure from Moscow's line. In 1965, party leader Gheorghe Gheorghiu-Dej died and Nicolae Ceauşescu came to power. The hopes for a better life eventually proved to be just an

Brancusi, The Endless Column *at Târgu Jiu*

illusion, since Ceauşescu pursued a hard-line neo-Stalinist policy, which skyrocketed after 1971. The last 15 years of his dictatorship were marked by arbitrary and megalomaniac decisions, the country's impoverishment and isolation, a plummeting standard of living, and the control of the entire society by the political police. That explains, in part, the violence that accompanied the popular revolt of December 1989.

Romania Today:
Between the Benefits of Democracy
and the Ailments of Transition

After the 1989 revolution, Romanians hoped that the country would quickly recapture its prosperity and would reintegrate in the West-European world. The multi-party system and the principles of market economy were reinstated, and a new Constitution was adopted (1991). But not before long Romanians became sharply aware that progress would be very difficult and time-consuming. An unbalanced and impoverished economy, the resistance of communist mentalities, the collapse of the Romanian markets due to the loss of former partners, and the failure to achieve rapid privatization and structural reforms in the economy raise important problems in everyday life. The slump in industrial production, inflation, the depreciation of the national currency, unemployment, as well as political manipulations, generated social tension accompanied by eruptions of violence (notably the miners' riots). All this has also affected the country's image abroad.

Still, many things have changed since 1989. It is true that Romania remains affected by the crisis of transition. However, life is different from ten years ago. The press, the radio and TV stations, the numerous political parties and the civic organizations approach society openly. The elections of 1990, 1992 and 1996 were held in a democratic climate, a proof to the fact that the institutions of the rule of law have matured.

Government

Under the 1991 Constitution, Romania is a parliamentary Republic. Political power belongs to the people and is exercised according to the principles of democracy, freedom and human dignity. Romania is governed on the basis of a multi-party democratic system and of the separation of the legal, executive and judicial powers.

Legislative power is vested in the bicameral Parliament comprising the Chamber of Deputies (343 seats) and the Senate (143 seats). Parliament is elected by universal adult suffrage for a term of four years.

Executive power is vested in the Government, headed by the Prime Minister, who is appointed by the President. Members of the Government are appointed by the Prime Minister and approved by the Parliament. The Government answers to the Parliament. In every county there is a prefect appointed by the Government.

Local councils and mayors are the public administrative authorities in towns and communes. County Councils are in charge of coordinating the activities of the town and commune councils. Mayors, local councils and county councils are elected by universal adult suffrage for a four-year term.

The President, who is also Commander-in-Chief of the Armed Forces, is elected by universal adult suffrage for a maximum of two four-year terms. Once elected, the President may not remain a member of any political party.

The judicial system comprises the Supreme Court of Justice, the Courts of Appeal, county and local courts and military courts. The Public Ministry discharges its functions through prosecutors constituted into prosecutor's offices. Judges obey only the law and they are irremovable. Judges and prosecutors are nominated by the Superior Council of Magistrates and appointed by the President. The Superior Council of Magistrates is elected by the Parliament for a four-year term.

Political Life

The downfall of the communist system was followed by a return to a democratic regime based on a multi-party system.

Bucharest. The Parliament Palace

Numerous political parties were formed and several parties – the inter-war National Peasant Party, National Liberal Party and Social Democrat Party - were re-established. By April 1990 more than 80 parties had been registered and by the time of the September 1992 elections, there were 91 registered political parties. During the parliamentary and presidential elections held on May 20, 1990, the National Salvation Front (NSF) achieved overwhelming victory and Ion Iliescu was elected President. In March 1992, NSF split into two factions, which later became the Social Democracy Party of Romania (SDPR) and the Democratic Party. Legislative and Presidential elections took place in September 1992. SDPR gained the biggest number of seats in the Chamber of Deputies and the Senate and Ion Iliescu won the second round of the Presidential poll. Fifty parties participated in the 1996 elections, but only a few managed to pass the 3% threshold allowing access to the Parliament. This time, the winner was the Romanian Democratic Convention, an alliance of political parties and civic organisations, which had been the main opposition force. The Christian Democratic National Peasant Party, the National Liberal Party (allied in the Romanian Democratic Convention), the Democratic Party and the Romanian Social Democratic Party, together with the party of ethnic Hungarians, the Democratic Union of Hungarians in Romania, formed a coalition cabinet. The Social Democracy Party of Romania, the Greater Romania Party and the Romanian National Unity Party made up the opposition in 1996. Professor Emil Constantinescu, the candidate of the Romanian Democratic

A debate in the Chamber of Deputies

Convention, defeated Ion Iliescu in the second round of the Presidential elections.

Foreign Policy

Throughout history, the major objectives of the Romanian foreign policy have been closely linked to the fundamental aspirations for a unitary and independent Romanian state. The Romanian countries, in the Middle Ages, fought (arms in hand, or by clever diplomatic means) to protect their territory and national being against the expansionist tendencies of neighboring great empires. Many a time, their efforts were successful, but sometimes they also knew failure. With the growth of national consciousness in the 19th century, the unity

Alba Iulia. The Cathedral of the Nation's Reunification (1921/1922)

of the Romanian countries became the primary target. Romanian diplomacy was instrumental in achieving the union of Wallachia and Moldavia in 1859 on the face of the great powers' opposition. The union of 1859 was only a step toward unity. At the beginning of the 20th century half of the Romanians still lived outside the boundaries of the 'mother country'. In the wake of World War I, the Romanians saw their long-cherished dream of a unitary nation-state fulfilled. The main objective throughout the inter-war period was to maintain the frontiers established at the end of World War I. Romania was an active member of the League of Nations and supported those initiatives intended to strengthen collective security and protect the existing national boundaries against revision. Romania heavily relied on France and Great Britain, countries regarded as main guarantors of political equilibrium in the region. A constant feature of the Romanian policy throughout that period was the support and adherence to all international agreements meant to strengthen peace and security. In line with this policy, the Romanian governments consistently promoted regional alliances. The Little Entente (Romania, Czechoslovakia and Yugoslavia) founded in 1920/1921, and the Balkan Entente (Romania, Yugoslavia, Greece and Turkey), created in 1934, were intended to provide security for the member countries. Their defensive character was manifest in the consistent support of disarmament and international agreements to outlaw war as a means of settling disputes. No picture of the foreign policy in the inter-war period is complete without mentioning the outstanding role played by Nicolae Titulescu, foreign minister of Romania (1927-1928). He was the permanent representative of this country to the League of Nations, and president of the international organization in 1930 and 1931. On the outbreak of World War II, all the efforts made to preserve the country's territorial integrity were crushed, and Romania, caught between Hitler's Germany and Stalin's Soviet Union, lost some of its territory and population to its neighbors. The aftermath of the war brought even dimmer prospects. Romania found itself isolated from its traditional allies of Western Europe, and, instead, included in the "socialist camp". For more than a decade, its foreign policy was built on instructions received from Moscow. The early '60s saw the revival of a relatively independent foreign policy. Although a member of the Warsaw Pact, it criticized and did not participate in the invasion of Czechoslovakia in 1968 and established links with western countries. Romania was the first socialist country, with the exception of the Soviet Union, to establish diplomatic relations with the Federal Republic of Germany, and the only one to maintain diplomatic relations with Israel after the Six-Day War of 1967. An active member of the United Nations (since 1955), Romania joined the activities aimed to strengthen peace and security in the region and in the world. The appreciation showed for the Romanian foreign policy wore out as it became obvious that, ultimately it was but another facet of the dictator's thirst for power and glory, and the openness, so much talked about in this field, was completely ignored in home policy. At the end of the '80s Romania was as far from Europe as in the grim '50s.

Timișoara, the city where the anti-communist revolt of December 1989 started

As of 1990, Romania's reintegration into European structures has become a major objective of the country's foreign policy. In 1993, it became a member of the Council of Europe, it was the first signatory of NATO's Partnership for Peace program (1994), and it became an associate member of the European Union (1995). Currently, intense efforts are devoted to increase regional cooperation, with special attention being paid to the Black Sea region. Treaties of friendship have been signed with Bulgaria, Yugoslavia, Hungary and Ukraine. In a crisis-ridden region, Romania has imposed itself as a factor of balance, stability and concord.

Romania's joining the European and Atlantic structures is not only the primary objective of the Romanian foreign policy, but also the choice of all political forces and the people. During his visit to Bucharest, in 1997, President Clinton told the Romanians to be confident, because the door to NATO "will stay open". The Washington summit, in April 1999, added more support to the Romanians' hope that Romania will be the next to enter NATO's open door.

ECONOMY

"Rich" has always been the word associated with the Romanians' land. Abundant mineral resources, rich soil, favorable weather, and clever and hard-working people have always been prerequisites for economic flourishing. Farming and sheep and cattle breeding were for many centuries the main pursuits. The country's location at the crossroads of major trade routes helped the development of trade since ancient times. Until late in the 19th century little changes occurred. The population was mainly involved in agriculture, which was heavily focused on grain. In 1913, 69% of the country's exports were in wheat, ranking Romania fourth in the world (behind Russia, Canada and the United States). Industries emerged and showed signs of development before War World I. Most of them were related to food processing, while the oil and petroleum industry, metallurgy and energy contributed less than 10 per cent to industrial output. In the inter-war period, industrial growth was fast and substantial in all domains. The remarkable development of the oil industry was stimulated by substantial investment of foreign capital. In 1930, oil production was almost 60 times that of 1918, pushing Romania to sixth among the world's producers. Methane gas production also placed Romania among the major producers of the world. Romania's economy continued to grow in the early '40s, in spite of the war demands. New roads and railways were built, agriculture saw significant development and the other industries also increased.

The establishment of the communist regime meant essential changes in economy. From the very beginning, the

Bridges across the Danube, at Cernavodă

Wheat harvesting in the Bărăgan Plain

Bucharest. World Trade Plaza

Bucharest. The National Bank of Romania

communist regime decided that one of their major tasks was to turn Romania into a heavily industrialized country. Moreover, the socialist pattern of "Big Brother" had to be faithfully followed. The first step was to nationalize the entire economy in 1948. In 1949, the Communist Party started the "socialist transformation" of agriculture, namely the collectivization of agriculture, a process that was completed in 1962. Central planning became the hallmark of the socialist economy. Ceauşescu continued industrialization at a faster pace, while agriculture was neglected. Emphasis was placed on heavy industry, as his pet idea was to make Romania a machinery exporter. His ambitious plans required investment, raw materials and a strong labor force. The use of foreign loans for investment in industry led to serious indebtedness. Savage exploitation of raw materials caused the depletion of domestic resources, and Romania resorted to expensive imports. The labor force was mainly recruited from the rural area, which proved detrimental to agriculture. Unfortunately, Romania suffered from the worst possible combination between the drawbacks of the socialist economy in general and the abnormally ambitious plans of a dictator. Ceauşescu considered the command economy to be the only means to achieve modernization. Decentralization, yielding results in other socialist countries, was inconceivable in Romania. In fact, quite often, centralization even meant whimsical projects

Bucharest. Hotel Sofitel

The dam of the hydro-electric station on the Argeş

put forth by Ceauşescu. His megalomaniac plans proved to be economic and social disasters. In the '80s it was his own vanity that prompted the decision to repay the 21 billion dollar foreign debt before it was due, which required inhumane efforts made by the people, and forced the economy into grave instability.

In 1990, when Romanians emerged from the communist dictatorship and opted for a market economy, they found that the economic disaster was much worse than previously thought. Reform began at a much lower level than that of the other former socialist countries. The governments after 1990 planned the restructuring of Romania's economy with emphasis on the role of market forces and private ownership. The first step was made in agriculture. Under the program for decollectivization, some eight million hectares, namely 80% of the agricultural land, was returned to its original owners and their heirs. In the absence of farming machinery, with an aged population left in villages, agriculture has not become a real economic force. In industry, measures were taken to dismantle command economy, to privatize industrial units and to encourage foreign investment, but the results were poor. Fear of the high social cost of restructuring caused a slower pace for reform. The political crisis in the region and the loss of the former external markets after the dissolution of CMEA in 1991 deteriorated Romania's foreign trade and increased the trade balance deficit.

Acceleration of reform has been the major concern in the last few years as the governments and the people alike are aware that economic recovery is dependent on it.

Integration into European structures is a target in the economic policy, too. In 1993, Romania signed an association agreement with the European Union, and a free-trade agreement with EFTA came into effect in May 1993. In June 1995, Romania formally applied for full membership of the European Union. In 1997, it signed the accord under which it joined CEFTA.

The Danube-Black Sea Canal, opened in 1984

Teleki Library in Târgu Mureş

SCIENCE

Romanian science and technology boasts trailblazers in various areas. Emil Racoviță (1868-1947), a member of the "Belgica" expedition (1897-1899) in the Antarctic, was the founder of Biospeleology. In 1920, he founded the first laboratory of biospeleology in the world. The inventor of sonicity (1912) was the Romanian George (Gogu) Constantinescu (1881-1965). Nicolae Paulescu (1869-1931), who in 1921 isolated a pancreatic hormone, was a forerunner in the discovery of insulin. Romanian scientists also made significant contributions to aeronautics. Traian Vuia (1872-1950) was the first to build an airplane in 1903. For the first time in the world, he flew with a heavier-than-air airplane in Montesson, Paris, in 1906. Aurel Vlaicu (1882-1913) was a pioneer in this field, too, and Henry Coandă created the first aircraft powdered by a jet engine. Hermann Oberth (1894-1989), a German physicist born in Transylvania, laid the theoretical foundations of the rocket's techniques and of interplanetary flights. In 1923, while living in Romania, he was the first in the world to design a two-step rocket for geophysical and meteorological research. The discoveries of Ştefan Procopiu (1890-1972), later called the Procopiu Phenomena and Effect, were considered landmarks in physics. Romanian Medicine and Physiology boast internationally known names as Gheorghe Marinescu, one of the first who applied the encephalography in the physiotherapy of the nervous system, and Constantin Parhon in the field of endocrinology.

Mathematics has a long tradition in Romania. Well-known names are those of Traian Lalescu (1882-1929), one of the

The Romanian Academy

founders of the theory of integral equations, Dimitrie Pompei, whose name was given to several functions, and Dan Barbilian (1895-1961), who made an important contribution to Geometry and the theory of numbers. In the '60s and '70 the Romanian school of mathematics was reputed all over the world, but in the last years of the communist regime most of these mathematicians emigrated. At present, they are working in various countries as university professors or researchers. As a matter of fact, the Romanian Diaspora includes many such personalities. For example, the 1974 Nobel Prize winner for Physiology, George Emil Palade, is a professor in the United States. It is estimated that over 2,000 scientists left the country during the communist regime and are working now in great universities around the world.

In the Humanities, Mircea Eliade (1907-1986) made a name for himself in the history of religion, and in the last years of his life he taught at the University of Chicago. Romanians Stéphane Lupasco and Eugenio Coseriu are well-known names among philosophers and linguists, respectively, all over the world.

The highest scientific and cultural forum of the country is the Romanian Academy, which was founded in 1866. In 1948 it was "re-organized" and placed under the political and ideological control of the communist regime. Notable Romanian academicians, particularly in Humanities, were purged. In 1990, the Romanian Academy regained its independent, scientific status. It comprises 175 members (86 full and 89 corresponding members), as well as 92 honorary members from 21 countries. The Romanian Academy has three branches – in Iaşi, Cluj-Napoca and Timişoara, with 66 research institutes, 26 of which were founded after 1990. The Academy's Library, with over 7,800,000 titles, is the second largest library in the country. Its publishing house puts out *The Annals of the Romanian Academy, The Memoirs of the Romanian Academy*, over 95 publications of the institutes coordinated by the Academy, as well as works of high scientific standards.

Education

The first primary schools existed within churches, while seminaries functioned within monasteries. In the wealthy families private tuition prevailed, with Romanian, Greek and, since late 18th century, French and German teachers. In the 17th century, in Wallachia and Moldavia, "Princely Academies", that is schools founded by ruling princes, covered the university stage. The teaching language in those schools was mainly Greek. Higher education in the Romanian language started in the first decades of the 19th century. Under the law on public instruction, promulgated in 1864, primary education became compulsory and free of charge. The first modern universities were founded in 1860 (Iaşi) and 1864 (Bucharest). They were followed by Cluj (1872) and Cernăuţi (1875). The communist regime extended state ownership over all education units. Illiteracy, which at the end of the World War II affected one quarter of the population, was eradicated through an intensive campaign, and compulsory education was extended to 7, then to 8, and later, to 10 years. In 1990, the first private schools were established. The number of private kindergartens, primary and secondary schools is still very low, but private universities are attended already by a quarter of the students. The reform of education is in progress, aiming at bringing it in line with the European Union standards. University autonomy has been in place since 1990.

Bucharest University

Alba Iulia. The Battyáneum Library (18th c.)

The education system comprises kindergartens (for children aged 3 to 6), primary schools (1st-4th grades), secondary schools (5th-8th grades), and high schools (9th-12th grades). Grades 1st to 8th are compulsory. Vocational education, as well as the training of apprentices and foremen, lasts 1-2 years. Higher education takes 4 to 6 years. There are 30,000 schools and higher education units attended by 4.7 million pupils and students (20% of the country's population); the teaching staff numbers 313,000 persons. The universities in Bucharest, Iaşi, Cluj-Napoca, Timişoara, Craiova, Braşov and Galaţi existed before 1990. After the 1989 revolution, new universities were opened in another 18 towns. There are 2,800 schools – primary, secondary and high schools – for ethnic minorities.

THE MEDIA

Censorship and the economic crisis of the last decade of communism resulted in a very poor landscape in the media. The number of central daily newspapers fell dramatically to only a handful, and local papers almost disappeared. The national television, which had initially transmitted on two channels for 20-24 hours a day, reduced its program to one channel, and broadcast only two hours a day. The activity of the 24 state-run publishing houses dramatically declined, and in 1989 only 1,900 titles came out, that is less than in the '50s and the '60s.

After December 1989 there has been a genuine information boom, unmatched by any other sector of the Romanian society. The transition from the absolute control by the Communist Party and the strict censorship of information to full freedom took place in only a couple of weeks. After 1990 there was an exponential growth in the number of newspapers and magazines, publishing houses, radio and television studios and news agencies – all in the private sector. Only the national news agency ROMPRES (f. 1949), the National Radio (f. 1928) and Television (f. 1957) Companies and a few other institutions are still in the public sector. There are about 1,320 newspapers and magazines, out of which 110 are dailies; 180 are published in the languages of ethnic minorities, particularly in Hungarian and German. In 1990, the circulation of the main dailies (*Adevărul, România Liberă, Evenimentul Zilei, Curentul, Ziua, Național, Cotidianul, Curierul Național, Libertatea, Cronica Română*) frequently exceeded one million copies a day, but today it ranges between 50,000 and 200,000. There are also dailies in English and French, like *Nine o'Clock* and *Bucarest Matin*, several weeklies, such as *Romanian Economic Observer,* the English version of *România Liberă*, *Romanian Business Journal, The Business Review,* and monthlies, such as *Curierul Românesc* (for the Romanians abroad). Over the past few years, local papers have also grown in number. Cheap illustrated weeklies or monthlies have seen a fast expansion, while interest in cultural and scientific magazines diminished. However, there are cultural weeklies like *România Literară* (30 years old), *22* and *Dilema* (founded after the Revolution) that have kept their faithful readers. The old system of state-run publishing houses was dismantled, and over 3,000 private publishers appeared, which produce over 7,500 titles per year, with a total circulation of nearly 40 million copies.

Besides the national news agency ROMPRES, there are other private agencies: Mediafax, AR Press, AM Press, etc.

The National Television Company, with over 13,000 hours of transmission per year, has three channels: TVR1, TVR2 and TVR International, with local studios in the cities of Iaşi, Cluj-Napoca and Timişoara. The private television channels, including the most popular PRO TV and Antena 1, transmit 56 programs nation-wide. The National Radio Broadcasting Company (with three national programs, as well as programs in 17 languages for listeners abroad) has expanded its transmissions from 60,000 to over 80,000 hours per year. Nevertheless it faces tough competition from the 140 private radio stations. The number of radio subscriptions is 4.2 million, and the number of television subscriptions is 4.1 million. As for cable television, its 2.8 million subscriptions place Romania in a leading position in Europe.

The studios of the PRO TV private television channel

CULTURE

The Source

The village was not only the space of a predominantly agriculture-based economy, but also the hub of spiritual life. The rich and still vivid popular art and culture draw inspiration from immemorial agrarian and fertility rites. Old symbols and motifs are discernible in the decoration of churches or pottery, as well as in literature, music or dance. The wooden churches are the acme of Romanian folk art. Their graceful simplicity and harmony, their exceptionally tall steeples made them famous worldwide. An example is the 18th century church of Şurdeşti, in Maramureş, whose steeple is 53 m. high, the highest in Europe.

Pottery, which dates back to the Neolithic, holds a distinct place. Two anthropomorphic statuettes unearthed at Cernavodă, in Dobrudja, belonging to the Hamangia Neolithic Culture, named the *Thinker* and *His Spouse* (5th millennium BC), are considered masterpieces. The Cucuteni painted pottery from the 3rd millennium BC is one of the world's most beautiful examples of prehistoric earthenware in Europe. Today there are tens of centers where potters still use traditional techniques.

Folk literature, with its great variety of genres, is the domain in which the Romanian soul is best expressed. Two Romanian ballads are considered masterpieces: *Miorița* (Ewe Lamb) and *Master Manole*. *Miorița* is the story of the shepherd who is told by a miraculous sheep that he will be killed by his fellows;

Painted bowl of the Cucuteni Culture (3rd millennium BC)

Dacian art (4th c. BC)

he is neither scared nor does he fight back, but he entrusts it with his last wishes, expressing a vision of death as a cosmic wedding. Though largely considered an epitome of the Romanian's acceptance of destiny, *Miorița* is rather a poem about the profound harmony between man and the universe. *Master Manole* is the story of the master mason who has to wall his wife in the foundation of the monastery he is building lest the construction should collapse overnight. Perhaps the value of these two ballads comes from the fact that they express eternal truths: that beauty and sacrifice, love and death are inseparable. The same idea can be traced in the lyrics of funeral customs, where moments of grief and cheerfulness alternate in the *bocet,* a lament for the dead, mostly uttered by women. Several such pieces have been included in the UNESCO archives as exquisite samples of the genre.

The Arbore Church in Northern Moldavia (16th c.)

Outer fresco of Voroneţ Monastery (16th c.)

The Mediaeval and Pre-Modern Culture

During the 14th-18th centuries, Romanian culture evinced two major trends: one towards the West and the other towards the Eastern Orthodox world. The first mainly sprang from the Romanians' Latin origin, but also from the political, military and economic relations with Central-European powers. The links with the Eastern Christian world were due first to their faith, and later, they were a consequence of the centuries long Ottoman presence in the area. After the Slavic eruption and emergence of Slav states in the Balkans, Romanians remained in the sphere of influence of the "New Rome," Constantinople, the capital of the Byzantine Empire. They came to be the only Latin people of Orthodox faith. After the fall of Constantinople, the Ottoman rule in neighboring

Gospel. Miniature by Gavril Uric (1429)

Prince Mircea the Old. Fresco at Curtea de Argeş (16th c.)

Prince Constantin Brâncoveanu and his family.
Votive picture at Hurezi Monastery (17th c.)

countries had a paradoxical effect. The Romanian princes, the only Christian rulers left in this region, extended their cultural patronage over the entire Orthodox world south of the Danube. North of the Danube the result was the development of a culture structured after the Byzantine model. Historian Nicolae Iorga summed up the situation in the phrase "Byzantium after Byzantium," meaning that Byzantium continued to live in the Romanian countries.

One or the other of the two mentioned tendencies acquired various forms depending on the region, the epoch and the field. Architecture reflected both trends for centuries, which resulted in interesting syntheses. Painting and music, of a predominantly religious character, were closer to the Byzantine tradition. This is obvious not only in frescoes, but also in miniatures, liturgical embroidery, and illuminations. A Four-Gospel volume, illuminated by Gavril Uric, the first Romanian painter known by name, in 1429, is now at the Bodleian Library of Oxford University. Mural paintings blossomed in the 14th century. The frescoes of the princely church of Curtea de Argeş (Wallachia), completed in 1362–1366, are among the best achievements. In Moldavia, during the reign of Stephen the Great (1457-1504), a "Moldavian style" of great originality and stylistic unity developed from combined Gothic and Byzantine elements. The monumental church of the Neamţ Monastery served, for more than a century, as a model for all Moldavian churches and monasteries. The style was continued in the 16th century, during the rule of Stephen the Great's son, Petru Rareş (1527-1538; 1541-1546). That was the time when the world-famous monasteries in Northern Moldavia (Bukovina) were built and painted: Moldoviţa (1532-1537), Voroneţ (1547), Suceviţa (1582-1596). Their exterior wall paintings represent the last flourishing epoch in the history of Byzantine art after the fall of Constantinople. Transylvania had closer ties with Central Europe. The Black Church in Braşov (14th-15th century), other cathedrals, as well as the Bran Castle in Braşov County (14th c.), the Hunyade Castle in Hunedoara (15th century) are monuments specific to the Gothic style.

For many centuries, the language of the church and of culture was Slavonic. The first printed book, a prayer book, was produced in Wallachia in 1508. The translations of the Gospels in the 16th century were the first written literary texts in Romanian. Until the 18th century, written culture mainly consisted of historical, moral, religious and legal writings, the authors being scientists rather than writers. Prince Dimitrie Cantemir (1673-1723), for a short while ruler of Moldavia, was an outstanding personality of that time. He was known in Europe as a remarkable scholar, author of writings in Latin: *Descriptio Moldaviae*, commissioned by the Academy of Berlin, a member of which he became in 1714, and *Incrementa*

Iaşi. The Trei Ierarhi Church (17th c.)

Church at Densuș,
Hunedoara county (13th c.)

Icon on wood (18th c.)

atque decrementa aulae othomanicae (The Rise and Fall of the Ottoman Empire). The latter, printed in English in 1734-1735 (second edition in 1756), French (1743) and German (1745), was a major reference work in European science and culture until the 19th century.

In music, Byzantine canons, touched by local influences, dominated for a long time. The monodic religious music, based on voices, usually without instrumental accompaniment, saw a period of glory in the 15th-17th centuries, when reputed schools of music developed in Romanian monasteries, the best known being that at Putna, in Northern Moldavia.

In the 17th century, impressive lay constructions (elegant mansions or sumptuous princely palaces, Renaissance-style castles in Transylvania), as well as great monasteries were

Alba Iulia. The Catholic Cathedral
(13th c.)

Arad. The Palace of Culture

built. Schools, art workshops and printing presses were founded in the monasteries, turning them into significant cultural centers. That was the time when the church of *Trei Ierarhi* Monastery in Iaşi was raised (1635-1639), an exquisite monument with its façades decorated with carved geometric motifs, covered with lapis lazuli and gold leaf. In Wallachia, especially during the reign of Constantin Brâncoveanu (1688-1714), an architectural style of a remarkable unity developed, by integration of Baroque and Oriental features into the local tradition. Splendid examples of this "Brancovan style" were the Hurezi Monastery in Oltenia and the princely palace of Mogoşoaia, near Bucharest.

Oradea. The Criş Land Museum, former Episcopal Palace (18th c.)

Modern Times

Beginning with the 18th century, cultural development accompanied economic growth and the political-national ferment. The Romanian society underwent a process of westernization and liberalization. On their way to the Western world, Romanians opted for the French model, which they pursued steadily and at a very fast pace. Urban life grew considerably. In Bucharest, the numerous French-looking buildings, erected around 1900, among them the Romanian Athenaeum, one of the capital's most famous buildings, were reasons to nickname the city "Little Paris". On the other hand, there was a drive to revive traditional elements of the

Măgura (Buzău county), open-air sculpture exhibition

Romanian architecture. Ion Mincu (1852-1912) was the promoter of the trend and the founder of the Romanian national school of architecture.

The first half of the 19th century was a time of great projects for the creation of a true national literature. The writers of the 1848 Generation pleaded for a sound and creative local literature drawing inspiration from folklore. Vasile Alecsandri (1821-1890) was a trailblazer in poetry, prose writing and drama, and he was also a collector of folklore. In the latter half of the century there emerged a triad of great classics: poet Mihai Eminescu (1850-1889), playwright Ion Luca Caragiale (1852-1912) and storyteller Ion Creangă (1837-1889). Eminescu is to Romanians the prototype of poet and of poetry. He was conversant with both Western and Oriental philosophy and, moreover, he was a great admirer of folklore. He gave maximum brilliance to Romanian Romanticism and radically changed the poetic expression by doing away with rhetoric. Ion Luca Caragiale's plays are a merciless satire of the Romanian society of the time. "Owing to the value of his comedies of morals and characters, unfortunately written in a language that does not have the advantage of international circulation, Ion Luca Caragiale is perhaps the greatest of the unknown playwrights", wrote Eugène Ionesco, the reputed founder of the theater of the absurd. In this time, Romanian painting made its brilliant entrance into modern art with the works of Nicolae Grigorescu (1838-1907), Ioan Andreescu (1850-1882) and Ştefan Luchian (1868-1916).

Between the Two World Wars

The inter-war decades saw an unprecedented effervescence of culture and the arts. It is doubtful whether any other period of Romanian culture saw an advance so comprehensive as that of the decades following the union of 1918. The period produced remarkable names in historiography, sociology, philosophy, literature and the fine arts.

Nicolae Iorga (1871-1940), an overwhelming personality, wrote hundreds of books devoted to Romanian and world history. The Romanian school of sociology was founded by Dimitrie Gusti, whose name is linked to the study of rural life through extensive interdisciplinary research. Lucian Blaga (1895-1961) and C. Rădulescu-Motru in philosophy, Vasile Pârvan in archaeology, made notable contributions in the Humanities. Literature flourished and produced successful innovations. Poetry gravitated around several great models: Tudor Arghezi (1880-1967), who materialized the abstract and ennobled the blunt expression; Lucian Blaga, who expressed metaphysical concerns in an expressionist poetry; George Bacovia (1881-1957), a symbolist; Ion Barbu (1895-1964), a representative of hermetic poetry (he was also a brilliant mathematician). Prose writings were in great demand. Authors were not slow to supply the public with novels and books poured from the presses. It was not, however, a sacrifice of art to business. Liviu Rebreanu (1885-1944) created the realistic and the psychological novel, Mihail Sadoveanu (1880-1961) wrote novels and short stories that are rather singular in Romanian literature owing to the metaphoric density and

Bucharest. The Village Museum

N. Grigorescu. Portrait of a girl   *I. Tuculescu. Grandfather*

infusion of Oriental wisdom. That period also saw a diversification of trends as never registered before. Modernism opposed orthodox-oriented traditionalism, while avant-garde groups denied all former poetical techniques. Tristan Tzara (1896-1963), the founder of Dadaism, Gherasim Luca (1913-1994) and Ilarie Voronca (1903-1946) started their work in Romania and later on made a name for themselves abroad much like Fundoianu (Benjamin Fondane, 1898-1944). Literary criticism and essay writing matched the development of poetry and prose writing. Standing out in this domain is George Călinescu (1899-1965), the author of a monumental *History of Romanian Literature*.

There was renewal also in fine arts. Constantin Brancusi (1876-1957) is acclaimed by the public and specialists alike as the founder of modern sculpture. Some of his works are in Romania: *Prayer* (1907), *Wisdom of the Earth*, and the ensemble (1936-1938) at Târgu Jiu, nearby his native place, the Hobița village. It consists of the *Endless Column*, the *Table of Silence* and the *Gate of Kiss* and was dedicated to the Romanian soldiers who died in World War I. They are Brancusi's only open-air ensemble of sculptures in the world. Romanian painting, which absorbed a variety of modern trends, saw considerable diversification and innovation. Nicolae Tonitza (1886-1940), Francisc Şirato (1877-1953), Lucian Grigorescu (1894-1965), Gheorghe Petraşcu (1872-1949) and Theodor Pallady (1871-1956) are among the best-known names. The Romanian avant-garde is represented by Victor Brauner (1903-1966), who later became famous in France, Marcel Iancu (1895-1984), as well as the abstractionist Hans Mattis-Teutsch (1884-1960).

The Romanian music school was already famous through Haricleea Darclée (1860-1939), who performed *Tosca*, when it was premiered at *Constanzi* theater in Rome, in 1900. It continued to be present on international stages, especially due to such performers and conductors as: pianists Dinu Lipatti (1917-1950) and Clara Haskil (1895-1960), conductors Ionel Perlea (1900-1970) and Sergiu Celibidache (1912-1996), who developed their careers outside Romania, or George Georgescu (1887-1964) and Constantin Silvestri (1913-1969).

The overwhelming personality of George Enescu (1881-1955), composer (his *Oedipus* opera is well known by music lovers), conductor and instrumentalist raised the Romanian music to fame. He was the teacher of Yehudi Menuhin and a close friend of Béla Bartók, the Hungarian composer born in a small town near Timişoara, in Romania.

Communist Dictatorship

During communism, the freedom of expression was constantly restricted, and literature and the arts were used as means for communist propaganda. The dogmatism of the '50s gave way to a relative relaxation in the '60s. Ceauşescu's

Wooden house in Oltenia

Ştefan Luchian. Anemones

Brancusi. The Kiss

C. Baba. Portrait of musician G. Enescu

"The Tempest" by W. Shakespeare
on the stage of the Hungarian Theater in Cluj-Napoca

dictatorship brought new pressures in order to impose a shallow and shrill kind of nationalism, especially during the '70s and '80s. There was a chasm between the official and genuine culture. The people perceived the outstanding works as a realm of moral truths, and their authors were held in high esteem. Never was there such an accord between literary criticism and public taste as the one in the last decade of Ceauşescu's dictatorship. Prose writers like Marin Preda (1922-1980) and Augustin Buzura, poets like Nichita Stănescu (1933-1983), Marin Sorescu (1936-1997) and Ana Blandiana were appreciated by both prestigious critics (Nicolae Manolescu, Eugen Simion) and readers. The same was true with the theater, where a number of stage directors made a name for themselves: Liviu Ciulei, Lucian Giurchescu, Radu Penciulescu, Lucian Pintilie, Andrei Şerban, David Esrig, Ion

"Jederman" by Hugo von Hofmannsthal
on the stage of the German Theater in Timişoara

*"The Danaides", adapted and directed by S. Purcărete,
at the National Theater in Craiova*

Cojar and others. Some of them emigrated. They enriched
the list of reputed Romanian names in Diaspora, like biologist
George Emil Palade, Nobel Prize winner (1974), philosopher
and logician Stéphane Lupasco, Mircea Eliade (1907-1986),
the renowned historian of religion, Eugène Ionesco (1909-
1994), the playwright of the absurd, who became a member
of the French Academy, and Emil Cioran (1911-1996), the
essayist, who is considered the greatest stylist in French
literature after Pascal. Music saw the emergence of great
composers, conductors and performers, instrumentalists and
singers, who received great acclaim here and in many places
abroad. The George Enescu Philharmonic Orchestra and the
Madrigal choir, both from Bucharest, are only two names on a
long list of international achievements.

*"Terminus Paradise", a film by Lucian Pintilie,
the special prize of the jury, Venice, 1998*

The Post-Communist Decade (1989 – 1999)

The post-communist years have been a period of both tests and difficulties. People's interest switched to areas that had been inaccessible: TV shows, politics, cheap books and magazines. Moreover, the cultural arena – subsidized heavily before 1989 – had to face the rules of a market economy. In the last few years the number of theatergoers dropped from 6-7 million in the '80s to 1 million and that of moviegoers shrank from 211 million to some 12 million. However, the crisis has not eliminated creativity. Romanian theater and music still win acclaim on various stages of the world, thanks to exceptional actors, stage directors and musicians. A new generation of writers has been emerging these years, determined to rebuild bridges toward Romanian readers.

SPORTS

Romania is perhaps best renowned for its gymnastics team, its tennis players, and canoeists. In no other field have Romanian athletes scored such success as in gymnastics. At the 1976 Olympic Games in Montreal, an enthusiastic public and massive international television audience followed breathlessly the unbelievable display of talent and skill of the young Romanian Nadia Comăneci. She won three gold medals, one silver medal, and one bronze medal. Indeed, Nadia succeeded in transforming gymnastics as a sport. She continued her legacy by winning three times Europe's championship (1975, 1977 and 1979), and in 1978 she became world champion. Nadia, however, was not alone. Since 1976, other Romanian women gymnasts entered the ranks of the world elite: Ecaterina Szabo, Daniela Silivaş, Lavinia Miloşovici, Gina Gogean and Simona Amânar.

On the tennis court, Ion Ţiriac and Ilie Năstase soared to the top of world rankings in the '70s. The latter captured the prestigious FILT Grand Prix in 1972 and 1973. Romania participated three times in the Davis Cup final, without managing to win it.

Historically, athletic achievement has always been a tradition in Romania. In the inter-war years, Romanian sportsmen registered the first victories in international contests. The first Olympic distinction, a bronze medal, was won in Paris in 1924 by the rugby team. A silver medal in horse racing at the Berlin Olympiad (1936) followed it. The first world champion titles were won in 1934 and 1936 (in bob-sledding), while in boxing Romania obtained the first European

Tennis player Ilie Năstase

title in 1930 through Lucian Popescu. In the '50s, Romanians were successful in women table tennis, target shooting, boxing, wrestling and weight lifting. At the Helsinki Olympic Games (1952), Iosif Sârbu brought home Romania's first gold medal (target shooting). In the '60s and '70s, women's track and field saw a period of boom. Between 1957 and 1961 Iolanda Balaş broke the world high jump record 14 times and won gold medals in this event at the Olympic Games of 1960 and 1964. In 1968, at the Olympic Games in Mexico City, long jumper Viorica Viscopoleanu broke all previous European, Olympic and world records. Lia Manoliu (gold medal in disk throwing, in 1968) participated six times in the Olympic Games.

The Romanian rowing and canoe-kayak have many records to their credit. Canoeist Aurel Vernescu won six gold, four silver, and one bronze medal at the World Championship in 1963. Canoeist Ivan Patzaichin, a Danube Delta native, was a four-time Olympic champion (Mexico City – 1968, Munich – 1972, Moscow – 1980 and Los Angeles – 1984) and won seven Olympic and world titles between 1970 and 1983.

During the communist regime, athlete achievement was considered "a state issue of national interest" and its goal, as in other East European countries, was to increase the international prestige not only of the country, but also of the regime. In terms of material infrastructure, this attitude was of great benefit. Significant investment was made in sports centers, supplies and equipment; two hours per week of physical training were compulsory in schools; moreover, schools with intensive sports regimens were opened. Stadiums, athletic fields and sports halls were built in the large cities. Large participation of people in sports was encouraged. On the other hand, all that was accompanied by a careful control and coordination of performance sports. Romanian sportsmen were denied professional status. After 1989,

Romanian athletics also entered a period of transition. The State's involvement has dramatically diminished, as have the financing sources. Yet the dynamism of the 45 specialized federations and the efforts of the Clubs yielded remarkable results. The 18 and 20 medals won at the latest two Olympic Games placed Romania 14th at Barcelona (1992) and Atlanta (1996), with four gold medals at either Olympiad. In recent years notable results have been registered by women gymnastics, rowing, boxing (Mihai Leu and Francisc Vaştag won a professional world champion belt) and, naturally, football. This sport has always attracted the biggest crowds. Romania was a competitive participant in the last three World Cup tournaments. At the 1994 FIFA World Cup, held in the United States, the Romanian team qualified among the first eight teams of the world.

Indeed, by the number of Olympic medals won this century, the relative standing of sports in Romania would be the following: gymnastics (51 medals, including 16 gold ones), rowing (29 medals, 12 gold), canoe-kayak (31 medals, 9 gold), track and field (26 medals, 9 gold), wrestling (32 medals, 7 gold), target shooting (13 medals, 5 gold), weight lifting (11 medals, 2 gold medals), and boxing (22 medals, 1 gold).

Gymnastics star Nadia Comăneci

Wooden church in Bogdan Vodă village, Maramureș (18th c.)

TOURISM

Few places in the world are blessed with the perfect blend of beauty and the picturesque that makes a country a tourist attraction. The adversities of this century – world wars, the fall of the Iron Curtain in 1945, the country's isolation during the last years of Ceauşescu's regime, and the painful difficulties of the transition – have placed Romania at the bottom of the list in regard to the number of foreign tourists. However, preparations have been made to be ready to receive guests. Three thousand lodging units, of which 900 hotels and motels can accommodate 450,000 guests. The country's location at the crossroads of many European roads provides easy access to any region by plane, car, train, or ship.

Any part of the country can meet visitation demands year-round. One can spend the summer holiday in the resorts strewn on the Black Sea coast, or in the mountain hotels or chalets. To improve one's health, one can choose one of 135 spas with mineral and thermal springs. What can be more exciting than blending the best cure with satisfying an interest in history? Băile Herculane spa, in the southwest, and Geoagiu, in Southern Transylvania, for example, date from the time of Roman Dacia. From Călimăneşti, famous for the springs with curative effects, bottles of water used to be sent to emperor Napoleon III. In 1893, the samples of mineral water from Călimăneşti-Căciulata won the gold medal at the International Foods and Water Exhibition in Brussels.

Travelers who love the mysterious atmosphere of ancient or medieval times can find numerous places that bespeak the greatness of the past. Rock climbing or hiking in the

Carpathians, hunting in forests rich in wildlife, angling in the swift rivers in the mountains or in the maze of channels in the Danube Delta provide many opportunities for a wonderful vacation in Romania.

Last but not least, one should not forget the hospitality of the people, the delicious dishes, which are a novelty for a foreign tourist, as well as the fine Romanian wines and the well-known *ţuica* (plum-brandy). From the smallest villages in the mountainous areas to the more affluent homes in different cities, guests are always welcomed.

Bucharest - The Capital

Bucharest, the most important urban center of Romania, is not only a tourist spot of prime importance, but also a gateway and starting point for tourist destinations across the country. The large parks and the string of lakes lend the city a distinct note of a "garden-city". Time has not radically changed the look of the capital, but only added fresh touches to the old face. There are still many quiet streets, with houses still

Buşteni resort in the Prahova Valley

The Episcopal Cathedral at Curtea de Argeş

beautiful, despite the signs of old age. The French-inspired buildings downtown, which once were a reason to nickname the city "Little Paris", shelter museums, banks and other institutions. The 16th-17th centuries churches in Bucharest should not be missed. In the Sfântu Gheorghe church, built in 1698-1709, the great ruling prince Constantin Brâncoveanu was buried. The Romanians consider him a hero; he was beheaded by Turks on the charge of being unloyal to the Porte and his four sons shared the fate because they refused to abandon their Christian faith. The National Art Museum displays the best works of Romanian painters and sculptors. At the art galleries one can admire and even buy paintings by contemporary artists who have already made a name for themselves, or by emerging talents. The open-air Village Museum, built in 1936 and considered the second most important in Europe (after Stockholm) is a fascinating place that showcases genuine peasant houses from all over Romania. The Romanian Peasant Museum conveys the Romanians' love for their roots and traditions. After the fall of the communist regime, the "House of the People", built during

Ceauşescu's dictatorship, now the Parliament Palace, has become a major attraction in Bucharest. The second biggest building in the world (after the Pentagon), it mirrors both the megalomania of a dictator and the toil and sacrifices made by common people. Adding to all this are several places nearby Bucharest: the Snagov forest and lake (on the isle in the midst of the lake there is a monastery where ruling Prince Vlad the Impaler was probably buried), Mogoşoaia – with the Palace of Prince Constantin Brâncoveanu, the picturesque monasteries of Cernica and Pasărea, the Băneasa Woods, and the Căldăruşani Lake and Monastery (built in the 17th century during the reign of Prince Matei Basarab).

15th c. fortified church in Prejmer village, Transylvania

The Romanian Black Sea Coast

The coast of the Black Sea is the main tourist area, considering the large number of Romanian and foreign tourists. The 50 km-long Romanian "Riviera" is composed of a continuous belt of 16 seaside resorts (some of them also spas), out of which some are in high demand: Mamaia, Eforie Nord, Costineşti, Neptun, Olimp, Venus and 2 Mai. While enjoying a vacation at the seaside, one can visit the vestiges of Histria, the former Greek colony, founded in the seventh century BC. Constanţa, the greatest port on the Black Sea, is situated on the place of another Greek colony, Tomis. A

Sinaia. Peleş Castle (19th c.)

significant monument here is the Roman edifice, with a fourth century mosaic of over 700 sq.m., preserved unaltered. The city's extraordinarily rich archaeological museum harbors a large collection of ancient objects. The statues of the goddess Fortuna, the protector of the ancient colony, and the fantastic serpent *Glycon,* a divinity worshipped in Dacia, still tell that the love of beauty and the faith had always been associated. The Roman, Byzantine and mediaeval epochs are well represented in this museum. One should not forget the Genovese lighthouse (8 m. tall) built in 1300, the Moorish-style mosque (1910) a.o. By night, the old casino provides an opportunity for fun. Moreover, the Black Sea coast includes natural lakes, whose mud is claimed to have curative properties. Lake Techirghiol, the biggest among them, has several sanatoriums built around it.

Mogoşoaia Palace (1702)

Fundata village, Braşov county

The Danube and Its Delta

The Danube springs from the Black Forest Mountains in Germany and enters Romania through a spectacular gorge. Drobeta-Turnu Severin, the first town the Danube meets after leaving the narrow corridor, was a large Dacian and then a Roman city. Still visible are some ruins of the bridge built in AD 103-105 by Apollodorus of Damascus, the great Greek architect, who planned Trajan's Forum and Column in Rome. The Romans used the bridge to cross into Dacia during the expedition against King Decebal, which brought them the long-dreamed victory over the Dacians. Before reaching the town

Baia Mare. The tower of the St. Stephen Cathedral (15th c.)

99) Marginea pottery (Suceava county)

Fortified house in Oltenia

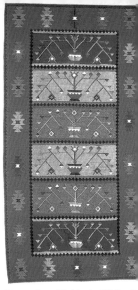

Carpet from Moldavia (19th c.)

of Tulcea, the Danube branches into three arms: Chilia, Sulina and Sfântu Gheorghe, through which it empties into the Black Sea. The three arms form the biggest delta in Europe (5,050 sq. km., out of which 4,340 on Romanian territory). It is a landscape of unsurpassed beauty, with over 1,200 species of trees and plants, the richest population of birds on the continent (more than 300 species, among which unique colonies of pelicans), and some 100 species of fish (from the Danube herrings to the caviar-producing sturgeons). Travelling by boat through interlaced channels and streams can be a wonderful experience.

The Danube Delta

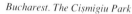
Bucharest. The Cişmigiu Park

The Black Sea coast

The Prahova Valley – Braşov Zone

The Prahova Valley is the most frequented mountainous area in Romania, with the greatest concentration of all-season resorts and spas. Sinaia, dubbed "The Pearl of the Carpathians," Buşteni, Azuga, Predeal, a. o. provide the best conditions for holiday and treatment to people of all ages. The low-pressure atmosphere and the clean air, as well as the beauty of this area enticed the royal family to choose Sinaia for their summer residence. The Peleş Castle, showing a Rennaisance style with Gothic elements, was built in 1875-1883. Poiana Braşov, lying in the immediate vicinity of the city of Braşov, is the most important resort for winter sports. Braşov is a great attraction for those who enjoy history and mediaeval art. They can admire the bastions of the old medieval fortress (15th-16th centuries), the old city hall and a lot of other old buildings, as well as Biserica Neagră (the Black Church), the greatest Gothic building in Southeastern Europe.

While in the Prahova Valley, one can make a lot of trips. It is worthwhile climbing to over 2,000 m. to admire *Babele*, huge rocks that look like profiles of old women, or the *Sphinx*, another natural rock that strikingly resembles the Egyptian monument. Not far from here is the Caraiman Peak (2,384 m.), where a huge cross was placed in memory of soldiers who fought in World War I.

Northern Moldavia

This area, known as Bukovina, is renowned for the beauty of its forested hills, the refinement of its folk artists, and the efficiency of its ancient spas (Vatra Dornei and Câmpulung Moldovenesc). The fame of its art monuments has long extended beyond the country's borders. Quite impressive are the five strongly fortified monasteries: Voroneț ("the Sistine Chapel of the East"), Arbore, Humor, Moldovița and Sucevița, most of them founded by Princes Stephen the Great and Petru Rareș. The churches, erected in the 15th-16th centuries, were painted in the 16th century, with outer frescoes that are unique in Europe. Suceava, a former capital of Moldavia (which in 1476 withstood the siège laid by Sultan Mehmed II, the conqueror of Constantinople), is a major tourist center of the region. From here the tourist can reach the Putna Monastery, built during the reign of the most important ruler of mediaeval Moldavia, Stephen the Great (1457-1504), or the Dragomirna Monastery (17th century), another telling example of the artistry reached in that field.

Maramureș

The Maramureș region, lying in the north of the country, in the depression bearing the same name, is surrounded by impressive mountains. Beauty with a capital B is an apt way to describe the view. This is a place untouched by time and history. In almost every village there is a gracious old wooden church with a high steeple. Most famous are those in the villages of Şurdeşti (with a 53 m.- high steeple, the highest in the world), Rozavlea and Bogdan Vodă. The peasant houses in Maramureș impress visitors by their monumental sculptured wooden gates, with intricate, delicately carved patterns. This old technique was handed down from generation to generation. Here, the folk costumes, the customs, and the songs have kept the tradition unaltered for centuries.

Tourists in the Doftana Valley, Prahova county

Poiana Braşov resort

Bran Castle (14th c.)

Săpânța, a border village in the northwest of the country, and a well-known spa for its curative mineral springs, is also appreciated for its traditional hand-made woolen blankets and folk costumes. A peculiarity is its "merry cemetery" where, on the beautifully carved and painted crosses, humorous comments about the faults and merits of the deceased are written by gifted villagers.

Southern Transylvania

Most of the mediaeval fortified cities in Romania are to be found in Southern Transylvania. Sibiu, Sighişoara, Mediaş, Făgăraş and Braşov were founded by the Saxon colonists who settled in Transylvania between the 11th and 13th centuries. Not only architectural monuments, but also streets and whole districts from the 15th-18th centuries have been preserved here. Churches from the South-Transylvanian villages, mainly those from Bârsa Land – Prejmer, Rupea, Biertan, Râşnov or Codlea – were turned into strong fortresses to protect against the raids of Turkish armies in the 15th-16th centuries. This is a phenomenon quite unique in this part of Europe. However, the biggest attraction is, perhaps, the Bran Castle, erected in the 14th century. To foreigners, this is the Castle of Dracula – the Wallachian prince whose merits were obscured by a malicious legend. To the west are the ruins of

Sarmizegetusa, the capital of Decebal's Dacian Kingdom and, nearby, of Colonia Ulpia Traiana Augusta Dacica, the capital of the Roman province, founded by Emperor Trajan in AD 106.

Northern Oltenia

One can find here picturesque mountain landscapes, karst phenomena (with some of the largest caves in Romania), spas along the Olt Valley (Călimăneşti, Govora, etc.) as well as numerous cultural and historical places of interest. Tismana and Cozia are the oldest monasteries in Wallachia, dating from the 14th century, while the monasteries of Arnota, Bistrița, Hurezi are remarkable examples of the flourishing architecture of the 17th century. A special attraction is the ensemble at Târgu Jiu, made by Constantin Brancusi, the greatest sculptor of the 20th century, who was born in the nearby village of Hobița. The *Endless Column*, the *Gate of Kiss*, and the *Table of Silence*, made during 1936-1938, were dedicated to the soldiers who died in World War I.

Besides these well-defined tourist areas, there are many other tourist centers, towns and spas in Romania. They include Iaşi (the former capital of Moldavia), Cluj-Napoca (the main town of Transylvania), Timişoara (the multiethnic and multicultural metropolis of the Banat), and Târgovişte (the princely residence of Wallachia, before Bucharest replaced it).

The Gate of Kiss, by Brancusi, at Târgu Jiu

CHRONOLOGY OF MAJOR DATES

1st millennium BC. The Romanian territory is inhabited by Dacians, a northern branch of the Indo-European Thracians.

70-44 BC. King Burebista, a contemporary of Caesar, creates a powerful Dacian Kingdom between the Middle Danube and the Black Sea.

AD 101-102 and 105-106. The Daco-Roman Wars. Emperor Trajan defeats Decebal and turns his kingdom into the Roman province of Dacia.

106-271/274. Dacia is a province of the Roman Empire.

1st millennium AD (latter half). The Romanian people come into being, as the sole Latin people in the eastern part of the former Roman Empire.

10th century. Documentary attestation of the first Romanian states. Already Christian at that time, the Romanians will be the only Latin people to belong to the Orthodox faith.

11th-13th centuries. Having defeated the resistance of the Romanian state formations within the Carpathian arch, the Hungarians include Transylvania into the Kingdom of Hungary, as an autonomous *voievodat*, until 1526.

1300 (after ~). Emergence of the Romanian feudal states of Wallachia and Moldavia. Accepting the suzerainty of the Ottoman Empire, they managed to remain distinct Christian states and keep their own institutions intact until the 19th century.

1599-1600. Michael the Brave, the ruler of Wallachia (1593-1601), conquers Transylvania and Moldavia. For the first time the three principalities inhabited by Romanians are united under the same authority.

1699. Under the Treaty of Karlowitz, Transylvania, a distinct principality under Ottoman suzerainty since 1541, is annexed by the Hapsburg Empire (until 1918). In 1775 the same empire will also incorporate Bukovina, the northern part of the principality of Moldavia (until 1918).

1812. The territory of Moldavia between the Prut and the Dniester rivers, called Bessarabia, is annexed by Russia (until 1918).

1821. Tudor Vladimirescu's revolution in Wallachia.

1829. The Russian-Turkish Peace Treaty of Adrianople scales down the Ottoman Empire's influence in Wallachia and Moldavia, favoring their economic and cultural orientation toward the Central and West-European world.

1859. Wallachia and Moldavia unite to form the Romanian nation-state, which adopts the name of Romania. The reforms instituted by Prince Alexandru Ioan Cuza (1859-1866) contribute to the modernization of the new state.

1866-1914. The reign of Carol I of Hohenzollern-Sigmaringen.

1877. Romania proclaims its full independence and joins Russia in the war against the Ottoman Empire.

1881. Romania is proclaimed a kingdom.

1916-1918. Romania participates in World War I on the side of the Entente.

1918. As the Tsarist and Hapsburg empires disintegrate, Bessarabia, Bukovina and Transylvania unite with Romania. Now all the territories inhabited by Romanians are united within the borders of one single state.

1940. Although it proclaims its neutrality upon the outbreak of World War II, Romania is forced by the dictate of the Soviet Union and Germany to cede one third of its territory and population. The Soviet Union annexes Bessarabia and northern Bukovina, Hungary annexes the northwest of Transylvania (until 1944), and Bulgaria takes the south of Dobrudja (the Quadrilateral).

1940, September. Following the abdication of Carol II (1930-1940), his son Mihai I is proclaimed king (1940-1947), but General Ion Antonescu establishes his own dictatorship and, in 1941, pushes Romania into alliance with Germany in the war against the USSR.

1944, August 23. Military coup d'etat by King Mihai I. Marshal Ion Antonescu is arrested, and Romania joins the United Nations, fighting against Germany up to the end of the war.

1947, December 30. With the Soviet troops on its territory, Romania enters the sphere of influence of the Soviet Union. The communists, who had gradually taken the power, force Mihai I to abdicate and proclaim Romania a people's republic.

1965. Communist leader Gh. Gheorghiu-Dej dies and his place is taken by Nicolae Ceauşescu, who institutes the most suffocating and destructive dictatorial regime in the country's history.

1989, December. A popular revolt overthrows Nicolae Ceauşescu's dictatorship and the communist regime. It establishes a multi-party democratic system and a free-market economy, paving the way for Romania's reintegration into the free world of Europe, with which this country has always identified.